THESE WORDS THAT
heal
OUR *Hearts*

NEYA B

Some ills can only be cured with words.

AUTHOR'S NOTE

This collection of poems is not a sequel to
"Poetry From Another World".

In this book, you will be confronted with many emotions, questions,
doubts, etc. If you can't handle this now, stay away from this book.

Take care of yourself, and live happily.

Do I sincerely love you?

I cherish you, touch you, and hold you close.
You, who say my name in that one, singular way.
You, who fill my soul with your affection.

But despite all this,
When I hold you as close as I possibly can,
Your scent filling my senses,
Making me drunk on this feeling the world so often exploits,
I wonder: do I sincerely love you?

And yet, it would seem there is no doubt.
My heart beats for you.
My body shivers for you.
My soul resonates with you.

Still, this doubt lingers.

Then I reflected, pondered, mused...

In truth, I don't just love you.
No, I love you far more than love itself.

That's why this doubt resided within me.

Because you see, this feeling has no description, label, or name.

It simply exists within my heart when I lay my eyes on you,
When I think of you, or even when my mind is empty of all thoughts.

This feeling is simply there, without any words or definition.
So no, I don't just love you, but it's far beyond love.
It's an indescribable feeling that will never have a name.

A nameless love.

Sometimes, we see that time passes
Without leaving our trace.
Looking back at our past,

We let it slip away,
Unable to act,
Leaving our soul to wither.

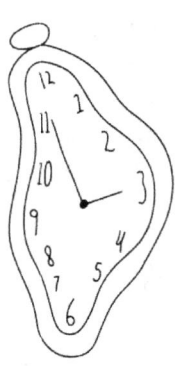

And sometimes, if they listened to us, would they see our wounded hearts? Would they understand the pain they cause us?

This blood that flows freely Turns our once pure souls to a deep, crimson shade.

How do I live with responsibilities that aren't mine?
Ones that tire me, drain me and exhaust me.

Since my youngest days, I played this role to please you,
Losing myself in emotions foreign to me.

But now that I know who I am and who I want to be,
I still wish to keep playing this role.

Only for you.

You, who carried me, cherished me and sacrificed all for me.

I will play this role if it can soothe your pains,
If it brings a smile to your face, lined by time,
If it brings you a moment of peace.

I will do it.

I will bear these heavy responsibilities until my last breath if it makes
you happy and proud.

Sometimes I feel nauseous,
For I am so fearful.

Seeing death close in,
I try to escape.

But these schemes are mere ruses,
Giving me a moment before my soul dissolves.

The deafening sound of rain hitting my window
Masking the sound of tears streaming down, soothing my being.

I am afraid.
Afraid of the unknown.
Afraid of this unknown.
Afraid of indecision.
Afraid of the unexpected.
Afraid of death.
Afraid of pain.
Afraid...

خوف.

Do all these fears make me weak?
Or do they simply make me human?

Under the relentless storm, I find comfort.
Its sharp flashes light the dark sky,
Its piercing sounds slice through nature's silence.

This chaos calms me, making me forget the one who fills my days.

They say the last child is favored,
As love fades over the years.

Fatigue grows, and indifference settles in.

اللامبالاة هي أيضًا معاناة كبيرة.

Some have wishes.
Some have words.
Some have actions.
Some have gestures.
And me? I have only wailing.

This longing never leaves me.
I hope to see you cradle my pains,
But your behavior makes that hope fade.

You, who were meant to be the source of my rest,
Have now become the reason my soul is exhausted.

Now, I find myself lost again.

في بضع كلمات راحتك هي السم.

All this darkness uniquely brightens my mind,
This chaos leads me to think that life holds much more beauty.

The hardness of trials has reshaped me,
Making me see the good even in the worst trenches.

"Everything comes in time."

I waited for you, but you never came back.

Your eyes are like an ocean,
Not by their color but by their depth.

Whenever I meet them, my soul dives in, never to return.
I think it's still there.

You are an ocean I love to dive into,

Losing myself until you choose to look away
Or close your eyes.
Those moments out of your gaze don't bring me joy.

For in the chaos of your emotions, I find peace.

عيناك مثل محيط الحب.

I am tired of being the one who understands everyone but never the one who is understood.

This automatic effort is never reciprocated, and it exhausts me.

Loving you didn't seem like a mistake.
But understanding you was.

الحب الذي يصبح أكثر الأخطاء إيلاما.

Imagining is no longer enough.
I am too old for all these illusions.
I need to live, to feel, to move.

But how, when loneliness only envelops me?

Almost 63 years ago, they would have thrown me into the Seine.

Today, some would be ready to do it again.

Will this endless loop ever stop?

Will we never learn from our mistakes?

شهدائنا.

Freedom is now only a conditional concept.
We are free only if we comply with the system.

Freedom is just a myth.
Freedom is only an idea to deceive the simple-minded.

The emerging twilight.

Those soft-colored hues
Remind me of the kindness in your words.
You were so skilled

At rekindling that dormant hope.

I realized I loved you when I prayed for you before praying for myself.

I never understood why I loved the rain so much,
That moment where chaos overtakes harmony.

The sensation of water washing away every emotion,
The feeling of a lighter heart.
The freshness of water against my skin.

I didn't understand.

But then, recently, I realized.

I simply find peace in that chaos.

Your sharp words seeking to pierce my flesh,
But the effects aren't as intended.

You want to see me cry, scream, lose control,
Yet I just look at you, my gaze empty of emotion.

Because yes, no one can wound a heart already dead.

كلامك مثل سيف ذو حدين.

This delicate touch you imprint on my skin,
Do you think it will always linger within me when you leave?

Writing soothes our sorrows,
Containing these complex emotions in simple words.

Transmitting a message from one soul to another.
It's a way to resonate together with an unknown heart.

A way to end the pain,
Which, in turn, is shared by many.

The pain of a heart is silent but destructively loud.

Poetry is a way for hearts brimming with emotion to speak,
Without being interrupted or misunderstood.

This fabric covering my body terrifies you,
But it is the source of my freedom.

الحجاب هو شكل من أشكال الحرية.

Solitude seems to be a blessing.
In its arms, we find comfort,
Until we fall into a bottomless abyss.

Until it becomes our only source of happiness.

But is it real? Or is it just an illusion?

Because when I'm surrounded by those I love, solitude feels ridiculous.

I still remember the sound of your sweet laughter,
The way you cradled me,
Your wrinkled hands applying henna on mine.

You were one of my sources of joy.
A ray of sunlight in this dark world.

Your gentleness still fills my soul to this day,
And your joyful moments remain my source of motivation.

In this world, I still hope to see you again,
But our souls will only reunite in the hereafter.

If you saw how I perceive you,
You'd think my eyes had gazed upon a masterpiece.

The moon's rays reflecting on dark water,
This chiaroscuro hypnotizes me, making me forget my torment.

بياض القمر هو راحة لا أستطيع أن أجدها في أي مكان آخر.

The softness of your words makes me believe nothing is ever truly over.

If I had the courage to say no, the courage to hurt you,
Would my life be different?

Away from the world, I find myself facing my demons.
Yet, after all these efforts, the only demon I see...

It is me.

الشخص الذي يؤلمني أكثر هو أنا.

Love is a sharp feeling.
Sometimes gentle, but it can easily become painful,
Or become a source of sorrow.

Love is a feeling to handle with care,
For one word too many, and it fades like a setting sun.

It illuminates the distant sky but is no longer visible,
Until the blackness of night takes its place.

Water is a resource that cleanses,
So why can't my tears wash away my sadness?

The sorrow of a heart is the source of an exhausted soul.

Emotions are like seasons.

Changing, repetitive, yet each with a unique power.

Some pass through you like a blazing arrow,
Marking any soul.
Others leave no trace as if they never passed through you.

But in the end, you are alone to face all these changes.

Your hands left marks on my body with invisible ink.

So, even if my words are heard, no one will believe them.
It's just us, witnesses to a silent yet vibrant moment of truth.

Empty that mind clouded by sadness, for radiant happiness can never pass through if you remain shrouded in constant darkness.

The night is a fascinating time.

When everyone finds rest, I come alive,
Letting my soul soak in this tranquility.

No living soul shakes the air with sound or movement; it feels like time has stopped.

As if to let the earth rest from being overworked.

This peaceful moment animates my soul, a simple embrace for this weary body, exhausted beyond measure.

I dream of seeing my brothers and sisters free one day,
Free from a murderous repression that robs them of every means to
live.

I dream of a day when we are all equal,
When our rights match theirs.

I dream that one day, their faces will shine with a light so bright it
would make the sun jealous,
A light that I wouldn't even be able to look at behind tinted glasses.

I dream of a free Palestine, plain and simple.

Suffering builds walls that are hard to break down. So take your time, and don't be harsh because the tenderness of a protected heart is a treasure to cherish.

Memories certainly create a sense of longing,
Wrapping us in a temporary world, already past,
But it's also a source of lessons.

A source that softens us but also strengthens us.

I would love to turn back time,
Change the world you knew.

But by doing so, would you be here today?
Would you be the person you are?

No one knows.

So why regret actions that weren't yours?

You had promised to love me,
To never abandon me.

Now I wonder where you are,
For my eyes cannot find you.

I have thus decided to love myself,
Because broken promises
Only feed this naive spirit.
While all your words were but empty.

Stars are remnants of a past story.
We still see their light after they're gone.

This makes me hope: since our love is dead,
Can we still love each other?

Or is that only reserved for light, able to travel for years just to be seen
for a fleeting moment?

Every beautiful thing has an end already determined; it's up to us to
prepare ourselves.

Time may divide us,
The world may forbid us from seeing each other.
Our words may never be heard,

But nothing can truly separate two souls meant to be.

I could never imagine a world without you.
Of course, you've occasionally been a source of my sorrows, but the moments of joy have been far more significant.

This world has ups and downs, but I want to live them with you.

الحياة بعيدًا عنك لا تبدو ضرورية بالنسبة لي.

I no longer had the strength to fight, and I wanted to give up as I watched my life go up in smoke.

I couldn't envision a future with this broken soul, but that glimmer of hope led the wounded child to believe that someday, we would make it.

And, thanks to that, today, we have.

The silent suffering of a heart is the loudest of cries.

The path to healing is not easy,
Nor is it painless.

It's a road that will break you more than the one that brought you
here,
But once it's over, your soul finds peace.

You are the treasure of my soul,
You dreamed I would come into this world.
And here I am to cherish and love you.

You are a part of my soul,
A piece of my heart,
A role model guiding my days.

I love you.

أختي المحبة.

Regrets appear like shadows on the walls.
My room becomes a place of remorse,
I can't remedy it.

Nightmares consume me,
While the moon nourishes these pains.

I look at its glow, thinking its beauty would distract me,
But all I see is the animation of my demons.

Letting this star set so the morning star may take its place,
Allowing me to sleep in peace.

Sometimes, to heal a heart or a soul,
Words aren't necessary.

Sometimes, we just need presence,
Or silence to find ourselves again after a deafening storm.

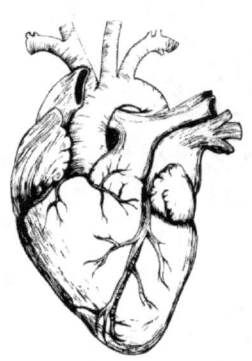

I thought that after spending part of my life by your side,
You would finally notice my distress.
But you were so focused on yourself,
That you didn't even see me.

Now, you look for me,
But how could I stay with someone who doesn't consider me?

When I look at the ocean, its irregular waves give me a strange feeling.

As if their movements uniquely lull my soul.

أمواج المحيط العديدة تهدئني.

I wish,
From the depths of my being,
The next generations will never feel this sensation.

This feeling of a dying heart.
This feeling of a soulless existence.
This feeling of an empty body.

This feeling of simply surviving instead of fully living.

The beat of my heart makes me appear alive,
But am I really?

You who watch me wander,
Don't you see that I am suffering?

A heart without a soul,
Is an unwholesome mix.
Yet you who look at me,
You drank from this mix and craved more.

I tried to push you away.

But now, once the battle is over,
I am no longer just a lifeless heart.

I'd like to thank you,
But you're already in the past.

– To this joyous soul.

Guilt shouldn't fill a heart victimized by others' wrongdoings.

قلبك الطاهر ليس مسؤولا.

Sometimes, a pressure wraps around my heart,
Leaving me nearly in agony.

I call for you, but even when I shout your name,
You're not here.

Then everything returned to me as if I was suffering from an emerging amnesia,
You're no longer here to soothe this aching heart.

For, in truth, *you* are its cause.

Melancholy is a sweet feeling in which I loved to hide,
Afraid of facing reality.

The smiles you brought me slowly turned into tears,
And into pleas on my prayer mat.

My soul finds peace when I please HIM.
Making Allah my ally was the best decision,
For now, I am at peace.

Your close ones complain about your roughness,
But what they don't see,
Is that you are the most sensitive soul among them.

Anger is simply a way to protect yourself.

The simplest encounters create the most beautiful stories.

I live without truly feeling,
Each day becomes a struggle.
My weary soul begs me to stop.

But this gentle breeze comforts me,
Reminding me that the beauty of this world still lies
In the hearts that surround us.

I couldn't explain it,
But the first time I met you, I knew.
I knew our souls were bound to connect.

A world without colors
Is like a soul without happiness, without healing.

It becomes monotone, seeking to blend into the shadows.

Being by your side wasn't just a meeting,
It felt like finding my place in this world.

As if I had found my home.

أنت منزلي.

The absence of a parent is like a missing puzzle piece.
Growing up, we try to fill the gap with each piece passing to feel
eventually.

Just to finally live.
To feel *normal*.

But as we grow, regrets only grow exponentially.

Healing, stepping back, helps us find the right piece,
The void we desperately seek to fill so there are no more regrets.

I would like to hols you,
To remove this pain drowning your heart and darkening your
thoughts.

Because I know how much your soul deserves a chance.

The most beautiful thing in all this,
Is that a dead soul can eventually come back to life.

يمكن للروح أن تحيا مرة أخرى في اليد اليمنى.

The harshness of your words hardened me,
Darkening this heart with layers of vice.

I fought to peel them away, one by one,
To make peace with the one and only version of myself.

The version that finally knows its worth.

This constant chaos that blurs my senses,
Will it never diminish?
Ever stop?

I'm beginning to suffocate.

So, seeing the torrent beating against my window,
I stepped outside.

For a moment, in the external chaos, I found a peace I had never
imagined.

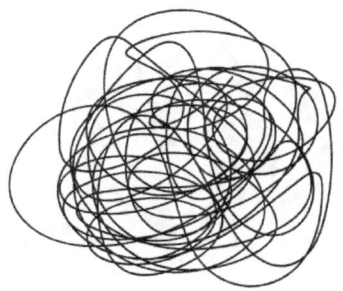

The most wounded hearts are the ones that cherish the small moments of happiness the best.

Every book has a first page,
Every story has a first chapter.

Every healing begins with a step.

It's up to you to write the next chapter of your story.

When I met your eyes,
Fear gripped my insides,
Shaking my already unhappy mind.

Then, time passed.

And now, when I meet them,
Nothing stirs within me.

Promises without worth are just words.
And words without action are just a waste of time.

Words sometimes escape me
When I meet your eyes.

I hope you know how to read my gaze.

I never truly forget,
I simply forced myself to forget,
To forget this pain that poisons my life.

Flavor becomes bland
When my heart becomes empty.

But these small moments of happiness
Bring almost new tastes.

The tears from your departure
Clouded my vision,
Leaving only sadness to feed my heart.

But recovering my sight, I realize
That the colors are only brighter.

دموع لم أرغب في معرفتها أبدًا.

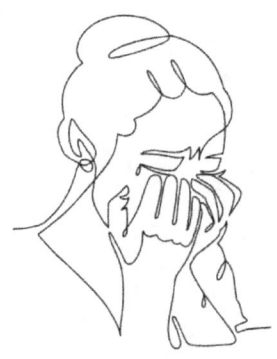

My body seemed devoid of any sensation,
Even the sharpest words no longer had any effect.

I thought I was disconnected,
Worn down by the years.

By reality.

Then I understood,
I simply healed.

The hours pass,
And I feel like I'm not moving forward.

They turn into days,
Into weeks,
Into years.

And when I look at the person I was,
There's indeed a chasm that separates us.

All good things come to an end.
And the bad ones, too.

His love was like armor;
I thought I was protected from everything.

But over time, it developed cracks,
Wounding me along the way.

Maturing is realizing that we can't stop people from hurting us, but we can stop reacting.

Sometimes, we think we don't enjoy physical contact.

But in reality, the discomfort is tied to the person giving it.

هل ستكون الشخص الذي سيغير رأيي؟

My past didn't make me "stronger"...
I just became more wary, anxious,
Always afraid my trust would be broken again.

I'm sorry it took me all these years to love you.

To show you what true, unconditional love is.
A pure and sincere love.
A love you deserved the moment you came into this world.
I'm sorry it took me over twenty years to get to know you.

To the little girl who dreamed of being loved.

When I was younger, I thought that not desiring to be in this world anymore was typical,
That we were all in a shared state of survival.

But no.

So I learned, listened to myself, fell, and got back up.

And that survival instinct gradually disappeared.

I'd like to thank you for your patience,
For the love it took me years to understand.

Thank you for the small efforts that went unnoticed.
For your unwavering support.

I'd like to thank you for simply existing.

Thank you, mama.

مفتاح جنتي.

I was designed to be the tough one,
The one who would receive and endure in silence.

The one people would confide their deepest and darkest secrets to,
trusting I'd keep them sealed.
The one who would comfort others as they cried, yet cry in silence
myself.
The one who always listened but rarely had the chance to be heard.

The one alone in this world of chaos.

A sore body seems more noticeable than a wounded soul.
Why this hierarchy?
To release you from guilt since you can't see it displayed?

Know that you cannot silence me,
Because even if you force me to be quiet before you,
My whispers are still heard in the heavens.

If your body reflected your soul, the sun would be jealous of your appearance.

Many made me want to leave.
And you made me want to stay.

If my breath stopped this very second,
I'd like to tell you that the pain would stop, too.

We can spend years suffering.
Then, at a particular second, a specific moment in this infinite time, it all stops forever.

Like a life drowned in an ocean of stories.

The ear of a trustworthy person is like a well where we can drown our sorrows.

أذن الشخص الموثوق به كالبئر الذي يمكن أن نغرق فيه أحزاننا.

Words are sometimes too much when expressing feelings.
So, let me show you how much you deserve to be loved.

"If their words didn't exist, would their actions be enough to show you their love?"

So, sweet words are nothing if actions are absent.
Don't be charmed by empty, falsely sincere words if your heart hurts.

Our mind leads us to believe that a cracked soul can never be loved in this world.
Our flaws would overshadow our qualities.
But in reality, one of those qualities will highlight the uniqueness of your soul in that person's eyes.

None of your flaws will measure up to your qualities.

The world can never tear me away from your gaze,
For it is one of the most beautiful things ever created.

You shouldn't be the collateral damage
Of another wounded soul.

They say that after death, the brain replays the best memories for seven minutes...

I think you'd make up most of them.

Some teach us that love isn't just a word.
We feel safe and protected as if that simple emotion shields us from a world full of chaos.

I hear your cries, but you don't see the hand I'm extending.

Nonetheless, I won't let you slip away when you're only a step away.

If I have to wait for a new world for your eyes to see me, I will.

What is a more beautiful sight than your eyes shining with hope,

Giving birth to a being free from all chains.

مثل الضوء في نهاية النفق.

Meeting a soul like yours made me realize that gentleness is not a weakness but the most beautiful strength.

My voice was like an echo in the forest,
Faintly heard, rarely listened to.
But filled with truth.

My soul was like a dead flower,
Water and sunlight may have been present,
But nothing allowed it to live.

Everything had to start anew
To become the most beautiful flower once again.

I count the days to see you again,
Because when I'm by your side,
I am no longer part of this world.

"In any life, I would have chosen you."

What joy it must be
To be the person chosen in every life.

Maturing is realizing that no matter someone's background,
It doesn't give them the right to hurt you.

I haven't lost my feelings for you,
I just realized you no longer deserve those emotions.

I can't explain when my soul began appreciating life; it simply happened.

Perhaps out of habit, perhaps because of my surroundings.
I don't know, but it is a joy to finally *live*.

If something or someone doesn't come back to you,
Then, it simply wasn't meant for you.

Words sometimes escape me,
While regret slowly seeps into my soul.

I wish I could sew my mouth shut so it wouldn't spill its sorrows
Into a well that doesn't fulfill its purpose.

Unexpected things often come that we don't know how to handle.

It's okay.
Even if you make a mistake,

There will always be a chance to make it right.

A wounded heart isn't afraid to love;
It's scared of being hurt again.

القلب المكسور لن يستطيع أن يحب بسلام إلا بقلب مثله.

Loving you seemed like a mistake,
But it taught me
To love the person after you better.

Finding one's place is a luxury few can afford.

Always wanting to please,
Never feeling worthy.
Making sacrifices that lead nowhere.

Thinking one's world is in ruins because everything sounded false.
Then, the moment the heart aligns with its surroundings,
It makes the body resonate uniquely,

Allowing that singular warmth to spread
And infuse our actions.

The heat of your arms makes me feel safe,
As if I had finally found my place.

A warm love.

A rejection shouldn't cost me a piece of my soul.

I'd like to tell you how much I love you,
To tell you how much you mean to me,
But out of fear, these words remain trapped within my soul.

Nourishing this infinite love.

I never thought
That love could heal
A heart wounded by it.

Sometimes, we think no one deserves our hearts,
But when it finds delicate hands holding it with love,

It blossoms.

Sleep was once my refuge.

I only dreamed of sleeping to enter this empty world,
Thinking it would soothe my soul.
But it only fueled my dreams, slowly eating away at my soul.

Now, I let myself bask in the sun's rays,
Imagining a life I wish to build.

The resentment that consumed my soul slowly turned into compassion,

Because you, too, were children brought into this world without a guide.

I will be patient with you, just as you were with me.

Your wounds are the source of your perfection.
Your scars tell me your story.

You have flaws that make you unique.
I wish I could show you that,

Show you as I see you,
But the only version you accept is the one you see in the mirror.

So give yourself a chance,
And you'll eventually see yourself differently.

The warmth of your caresses still lingers
In the darkest corners of my soul.
I hide them, hoping I'll never need them.

But each time I find myself at my lowest,
I find comfort in thinking of that gentle warmth.

A soul needs rest
When the world offers it no respite.

هل ستكون راحتي؟

Mending a broken heart is a hard, if not impossible, task.

You might have to give yours in its place
For it to work again.

صوت القلب المكسور يتردد صداه إلى ما لا نهاية عندما تشفيه روح فارغة من الحب.

137

A broken heart changes a person forever.

Looking back at my past, I wouldn't change any of it.

Yes, it left open wounds that I struggled to close, but it also helped me choose the right people to keep close.

Suffering is indeed painful,
But it makes us more discerning.

Healing is only found in your arms.

If someone asked me to describe my love for you,

I would say that only your eyes make me travel.
That only your words make me shiver.
That only your touch animates me.
And that just seeing you envelops my soul in a sense of tranquility.

One step at a time,
It's through consistency and discipline
That we manage to move forward.

Under the blue sky of a beautiful summer,
I thought I'd see you by my side again.
The wait was long on the fine sand,
But I couldn't cross paths with you again.

So, I let the waves cradle me,
In the hope of finding you.

I never thought life could change so much after entirely trusting Him.

It took me a while to accept the concept of *Tawakkul*, but now, it guides my daily life.

الثقة بالله غيرت كل شيء.

I hope my children never experience the suffering I knew.

I hope they'll never know the consequences of a broken heart.

In every story, there's a beginning and an end.
I knew that but never thought the end would be so near.

This world leaves us to struggle
Without a way out.

We are like newborns
Struggling to take our first breath,
Our heads are barely above water.

In murky water, dragging us down into the depths.

You who read this, your soul deserves unconditional love, healing every open wound.

ACKNOWLEDGEMENT

I want to say thank you for reading, encouraging, and giving me strength when I'm at my lowest. I tried to return the favor to you, who are reading this.

New stories soon. I love you. And take care of your heart and your soul.